VICTORIAN INDIA IN FOCUS

Frontispiece *(overleaf)*
Lord and Lady Curzon at a
tiger hunt during a visit to the
Nizam of Hyderabad in 1902.
A man of considerable intel-
lect, energy and ambition,
Curzon was possibly the least-
liked but most respected of all
the Viceroys. The steel corset
he was compelled to wear to
correct his spinal curvature
gave his figure an aspect of
relentless rectitude. He cared
deeply for Indian culture and
the preservation of her ancient
monuments. He founded the
Victoria Memorial in Calcutta,
a museum dedicated to British
rule in India, especially during
the Victorian era.

INDIA OFFICE LIBRARY AND RECORDS

Victorian India in Focus

*a selection of early photographs
from the collection in the
India Office Library and Records*

Ray Desmond

LONDON
HER MAJESTY'S STATIONERY OFFICE

Designed by HMSO Graphic Design

ISBN 0 11 580227 4

Printed in England for Her Majesty's Stationery Office
by W S Cowell Ltd, Ipswich
Phototypeset by Hugh Wilson Typesetting, Norwich
Dd. 716906 C15

Contents

Introduction

My interest in the early days of photography in India was roused when I saw for the very first time the large and varied collection of photographs in the India Office Library. My respect and admiration for the work of these pioneer photographers grew as I began to have some idea of the difficulties under which they worked. It was not just the primitive cameras and cumbersome ancillary equipment they had to use but also the technical problems peculiar to photography in the tropics which they had to solve. Yet frequently they succeeded in producing work that stands comparison with the best of European photography of that time. Some qualify as works of art and all are powerful records of the contemporary scene, so often communicating with greater impact than the written word the wonder and the excitement felt by English men and women living and working in the exotic world of India.

I have selected photographs which illustrate people, places and events and also some which, I hope, convey a feeling of the quality of life in India in Victorian times. Although the title of this book mentions only India I have included a few Burmese photographs and one of Ceylon for no other reason than that they appeal to me and I would like others to enjoy them as well.

All the photographs are reproduced by permission of the Director of the India Office Library and Records.

The Indian Scene

Europeans are either captivated or repelled by India; few remain indifferent. Its vastness alone encompassing every kind of geological formation from plains and deserts to hills and mountains commands instant respect. Its tide of humanity and multiplicity of tongues can be overwhelming and the stark contrast between opulence and poverty disturbing. Flimsy huts or bustees are uneasy neighbours of magnificent palaces and temples. The sub-continent is a palimpsest of many cultures and their artefacts: Buddhist caves at Ajanta, Akbar's deserted city at Fatehpur Sikri, Hindu erotic sculpture at Khajuraho, Jain temples on Mount Abu and Victorian buildings at Bombay.

To Europeans with artistic talents the visual appeal of this exotic landscape has always been irresistible. In spare moments officials of the East India Company would eagerly sketch a pretty scene or an interesting ruin while their wives and daughters would record a colourful bird or flower in delicate watercolours. Back in England there was a popular demand for views of India, which artists like Thomas and William Daniell were quick to exploit. From 1786 to 1794 they travelled India from the Himalayas to Travancore in search of the picturesque. Their enormous output of watercolours, however, could not have been achieved without the mechanical aid of the camera obscura, which artists since the time of Canaletto had found useful in noting detail and in resolving the problems of perspective. It consisted of a box of variable size with a small convex lens through which the subject was focused on to an inclined mirror and thence on to a sheet of paper on the base of the box. The artist could then quickly and accurately trace the outlines of the reflected subject, which would serve as a basis for a finished drawing. It was the desire of W.H. Fox Talbot at Lacock Abbey in the 1830s to capture in a permanent form the transient image of the camera obscura that led to his inventing photography using paper negatives.

It is doubtful if it will ever be known when a camera was first used in India but it is not unreasonable to suppose that it happened within a few years of its invention in Europe. In the summer of 1844 F.M. Montairo announced in Calcutta that he was 'prepared to take likenesses by the Daguerreotype process'. Patented by the Frenchman Louis Daguerre in 1839, the method involved using silvered copper plates sensitized with iodine and bromine but its main drawback was that every photograph was unique and could not be duplicated. Fox Talbot's use of light-sensitive paper employing a negative-positive process resolved this difficulty and calotypes, as he called them, were widely used in India until they were eventually superseded by the collodion process. In 1855 a correspondent to the *Photographic Journal* enthusiastically advised 'Indian photographers ... to turn more of their attention to the 'calotype' process which is so simple and certain in its effects.'

Officers and surgeons were among the first to take up photography in India. John McCosh, a surgeon on the Bengal Establishment of the East India Company's army,

> strongly recommended every assistant-surgeon to make himself master of photography in all its branches, on paper, on plate glass, and on metallic plates. I have practised it for many years, and know of no extra professional pursuit that will more repay him for all the expense and trouble (and both are very considerable) than this fascinating study – especially the new process by Collodion for the stereoscope. During the course of his service in India, he may make such a faithful collection of representations of man and animals, of architecture and landscape, that would be a welcome contribution to any museum.
>
> *Advice to Officers in India* London, 1856, 7

Within a year of its foundation in 1854 the Bombay Photographic Society had recruited nearly two hundred members and two years later similar

Silver zenana carriage belonging to Gaekwar of Baroda

societies were formed in Madras and Calcutta. From their inception these societies published journals and held regular exhibitions of their members' photographs. Photographic studios opened up in the main cities and in 1857, Messrs Johnson and Henderson, commercial photographers in Bombay, launched the first number of the *Indian Amateurs' Photographic Album*, which appeared monthly with three photographs pasted in each issue. This growing popularity of photography caused Samuel Bourne, newly arrived in India in 1863, to exclaim lyrically that 'from the untrodden snows of the Himalayas to the burning shores of Madras the camera is now a familiar object.'

Back in England it became apparent to the Court of Directors of the East India Company that the camera could be a useful instrument in the execution of its business. From 1855 cadets at its Military Seminary at Addiscombe received instruction in photography and cameras were despatched to units of the army serving in India. Engineers were encouraged to keep a photographic record of the progress of public works projects. It was even suggested that photographs of native pensioners should be attached to their identification papers to circumvent widespread fraudulent impersonation, a proposal strongly resisted by the Accountant-General, who was alarmed by the enormous cost of photographing all pensioners. Dr Norman Cheevers, Secretary to the Medical Board at Fort William in Calcutta, foresaw the usefulness of the camera in criminal investigations and confidently predicted that no murderer would ever face looking at a photograph of the

> actual scene of his atrocity – the familiar walls, the charpoy, the ghastly faces – as they last appeared to his reeling vision – the sight which has haunted his brain every hour since the act was done – while he believed to certainty, that its reality could never come before his eyes again.
> *Manual of Medical Jurisprudence for Bengal and the North-Western Provinces.*
> Calcutta, 1856, 40 – 41

In its issue for 11 February 1859 the *Photographic News* in London reviewed some of the latest numbers of the *Indian Amateurs' Photographic Album*. It singled out for especial praise a photograph of the Ellora Caves as 'a good example of what can be done by this art to rescue from "the tooth of time and the razure of oblivion" the monuments which abound in India of past greatness, and a zealous though deluded and misdirected piety.' On representation from the Royal Asiatic Society, the East India Company instructed that important ancient monuments in the territories it administered be examined and recorded. When, for instance, it learnt about the deteriorating state of the splendid murals in the Ajanta Caves, Captain Robert Gill of the Madras Army was sent there to make copies of them. After years of painstaking copying with pencil and brush Gill enlisted the aid of the camera and a selection of his photographs appeared in *The Rock-cut*

Temples of India and *One Hundred Stereoscopic Illustrations of Architecture and Natural History in Western India*, both published in London in 1864. The author, James Fergusson, believed that

> these photographs tell their own story far more clearly than any form of words that could be devised, and even without the text they form by far the most perfect and satisfactory illustration of the ancient architecture of India which has yet been presented to the public.

In a despatch to India in 1855 the East India Company directed

> attention to photography as a means by which representations may be obtained of scenes and buildings, with the advantages of perfect accuracy, small expenditure of time and moderate cash. We have recently desired the Government of Bombay to discontinue the employment of draughtsmen in the delineation of antiquities of Western India, and to employ photography instead, and it is our desire that this method be generally substituted throughout India, in cases where it may be considered desirable by the Government to obtain representations of objects of interest. We shall be prepared to forward the necessary apparatus for the use of any of our Governments which may make application for them.

Under this authority the Bombay Presidency seconded Captain T. Biggs of the Bombay Artillery to the photographing of buildings, sculptures and inscriptions in Western India. The following year Captain Linnaeus Tripe of the 12th Regiment Native Infantry, recently returned to his regiment from an attachment as photographer with the British Mission to Burma, was appointed to similar duties in the Madras Presidency. Valuable though such photographic surveying was, it needed to be incorporated into a comprehensive plan for the whole of British India. The first steps were taken with the appointment in December 1861 of General Alexander Cunningham as Director of Archaeology but the four years he initially held the post were too short to achieve much. In 1867, at the instigation of the Secretary of State for India, all provincial governments in India were reminded of 'the desirability of conserving ancient architectural structures or their remains, and other works of art in India, and of organizing a system for photographing them'. At that time the work of amateur photographers was gladly accepted but later it was decided that normally only the work of professional photographers would qualify for inclusion. Copies of these photographs were sent to the India Museum at the India Office in London, which used a selection of them in the archaeological reports it published.

Some particularly fine photographs of architectural detail appear in *Photographs of Architecture and Scenery in Gujarat and Rajputana*, which Bourne and Shepherd published in 1874. This firm was pre-eminent among the commercial photographic establishments in the sub-continent and its most distinguished member was Samuel Bourne. It began as a partnership between Charles Shepherd and A. Robertson in Agra in 1862 and opened

3

up in Simla two years later. There were already other commercial photographers established in this hill station: T. Reinecke, who also had a studio in Calcutta, and C.W. Rusett, who had abandoned the trade of habit-making for what he hoped was the more lucrative business of photography.

Samuel Bourne, a former clerk in Messrs Moore and Robinson's Bank in Nottingham, arrived in Calcutta in January 1863, a competent but obscure photographer. As Calcutta, the seat of Government in British India, with its stuccoed European buildings left him unimpressed, he resolved to go to Simla 1200 miles to the north. *En route* he paused at Benares, where he witnessed with horror the public burning of the dead along the banks of the sacred Ganges.

> Five or six savage-looking men were heaping wood on the blazing piles, but I could discern through the flames the roasting skull and feet of one of the bodies. One of them was that of a woman, whose husband stood by evidently regarding the horrid spectacle with the highest satisfaction.

He was predictably moved by the ethereal beauty of the Taj Mahal at Agra but Mughal Delhi evoked little more from him than a few remarks about the recent Mutiny. A glimpse of the blue haze of the distant Himalayas after a dreary fortnight travelling across the monotonously flat plains above Delhi raised his expectations. But Simla with its huddle of plain bungalows clinging precariously to steep slopes disappointed him. 'Its great defect to the photographer is its lack of water', he lamented. There were no lakes or rivers, only here and there a meandering stream. Like the Daniells nearly a hundred years earlier, Bourne was seeking the picturesque and looked in vain for rustic bridges and ivy-clad ruins. He was convinced that Indian landscapes could never stand comparison with English scenery.

> I have no doubt that in some parts of the Himalayas grand and striking views are to be found, as I hope ere long to verify; but they would consist chiefly of ravines, passes, and mountain ranges – without verdure, without foliage, and without water, and a photograph minus these three elements must possess very striking compensation features indeed to render it a pleasing and enjoyable picture.

He added without much conviction:

> I am told that in some parts of Central India, and near to Bombay, there is good rock and river scenery, which I sincerely wish may be true.

Bourne came to India equipped with wet-plate apparatus patented by Frederick Scott Archer in 1851. Negatives were produced on glass plates coated with a solution of iodized collodion and sensitized just before exposure in a bath of silver nitrate. The plate, still wet during its exposure in the camera, was immediately developed and fixed. Since wet plates required shorter exposure time than either calotypes or daguerreotypes,

and produced prints with finer detail, they soon superseded them, remaining the standard process until the 1880s. But the advantages of increased sensitivity and shorter exposure time were not achieved without new problems. Glass plates were easily broken, especially when they were being transported over primitive Indian roads; moreover, the outdoor photographer had his mobility impeded by all the extra equipment he had to carry, not least a portable tent for developing the plates. Some photographers also believed that collodion could deteriorate during its shipment from England. This was not Bourne's experience but he did discover that in a tropical climate the ether in the collodion evaporated too rapidly to permit a smooth and easy coating of the glass plate. For some time he was also puzzled by spots that persistently covered his prints when they were not present on his negatives. After deducing the cause to be excessive dryness in his stock of albumenized paper, he employed the simple expedient of dampening the paper before use to banish the spots.

When the rains put a stop to his photographic activities, Bourne decided to escape into the higher regions of the Himalayas. With a party of thirty porters to carry his camera and provisions, he left Simla in July 1863 on the first of his three Himalayan expeditions, which he reported in long enthusiastic letters to readers of the *British Journal of Photography* in issues spread over 1864 to 1870. A fairly easy road took him through forests of deodars, over mountain ranges and near spectacular waterfalls. He took personal risks to get photographs that would convey something of the sublimity of the landscape, aware at the same time that it was 'altogether too gigantic and stupendous to be brought within the limits imposed on photography.'

He paused at the top of Tarree Pass, which led to Wanga Valley, to photograph an enormous glacier pitted with huge boulders and rocks. While waiting for a blizzard to abate, he laboriously coated a plate with collodion but the intense cold prevented it from setting. The print he managed to make was disappointing but, nevertheless, he kept it because at that time it represented the highest altitude (over 15000 feet) at which any photographs had been taken. Frightened by the severity of the weather, his porters deserted him and Bourne later admitted that 'all my enthusiasm in photography and my great desire to see the mysteries of nature at high altitudes would not have urged me to this undertaking had I known what awaited me.' When, after three days on his own, fresh porters miraculously appeared, he descended into Wanga Valley, where, in good weather and with clumps of tall trees against the backdrop of mountains, he took some of his finest scenic photographs. After ten weeks he returned to Simla with one hundred and forty-seven negatives of scenery that had never been photographed before, his only loss being one broken ground-glass.

Bourne's next expedition, which was far more ambitious, took him as far as Kashmir and lasted nine months. This time he had his gear packed in smaller and lighter parcels. The biggest was his portable darkroom, a pyramidal tent 10 feet high by 10 feet square at the base; the rest comprised a large stock of glass plates (two hundred and fifty 12 by 10 inches and four hundred 8 by 4½ inches) and boxes of chemicals – in all twenty loads; his personal baggage and provisions made up the rest. Forty-two porters were recruited in addition to a retinue of personal servants and six dandy (i.e. portable hammock) bearers. He left Lahore in March 1864 and at the very outset of his journey almost lost his life through drowning.

The Raja of the small hill state of Chamba showed Bourne his large collection of cameras, lenses and chemicals with childish pleasure. 'I was surprised to find photography amongst his fancies,' remarked Bourne; 'it shows to what remote and hidden corners the camera has gone and collodion found its way.' Continuing his trek to Kashmir, Bourne followed a route little used by Europeans. Increasing familiarity with the Himalayan ranges did nothing to change his opinion that they lacked the romantic spirit of the Swiss and Italian Alps. He frequently regretted the limitations of the camera, especially at sunset when a 'purple indistinctness' flooded the valleys below and the mountains were starkly silhouetted against the glowing sky.

> How often have I lamented that the camera was powerless to cope with these almost ideal scenes, and that with all its truthfulness it can give no true idea of the solemnity and grandeur which twilight in a vast mountainous region reveals partly to the sense and partly to the imagination.

His first sight of the Vale of Kashmir from the summit of a high ridge, revealed as a gleam of lake water shimmering in the haze, was yet another ecstatic moment for him.

During the steep descent to the valley floor, his porters dropped a box breaking most of its 12 by 10 inches glass plates. Bourne hoped he might be able to salvage enough pieces of glass to recut twelve or eighteen pieces for his 8 by 4½ inches camera. Another setback was the discovery that the surfaces of some of his best negatives were crazed with a mass of lines, which he could only explain as due to the interaction of damp and high temperatures.

In Srinagar Bourne at last found the picturesque ingredients missing from the Himalayan panoramas: quaint bridges and wooden houses that 'lean and slant in all directions as though only waiting for a push to topple over.' He was entranced by Dal Lake with small boats drifting gently on its quiet surface. For two months he worked in perfect weather recording these idyllic scenes. When his supply of chemicals and glass plates was almost exhausted, Bourne began the eight weeks' journey back to Simla, where he saw for the first time prints of some of the five hundred negatives he had taken on this expedition and also learnt that the Bengal Photographic Society

had awarded him its gold medal for the best series of ten and its silver medal for the best single print.

He left Simla again in July 1866 on his last photographic foray into the Himalayas; this time the source of the Ganges was his destination. He found more than enough picturesque houses in the Kulu Valley for his photographic compositions. Climbing the mountains at the eastern end of the valley, Bourne always halted at any beguiling view. Out would come his camera and portable darkroom but by the time he had set them up the view would often be shrouded in mist.

> Ah you gentlemen! and you, careless public! who think that landscape photography is a pleasant and easy task – a sort of holiday pastime – look at me toiling up that steep ascent in the grey dawn of a cold morning in fear and trembling that my labour would be all in vain! See me sitting for ten mortal hours, shivering in cold and mist, on the top of that bleak pass, waiting for a 'break' which would *not* come! See me descending next day and go through the same again and say if *this* is a pleasant pastime!

At Dankhar near the Spiti River, the natives, the dirtiest he had encountered, lived in picturesque caves on the hillside. Smartly he set up his camera near one of their dwellings.

The Dal canal at Srinagar in Kashmir. Photograph by Samuel Bourne

The stench all around was so great, though I was close to the doors of the houses, that it was with difficulty I could get through the operation of preparing a plate; and when I came to develop it, lo! and behold! it fogged all over instantly, from the ammonia and other noxious fumes with which the air was reeking. Immediately suspecting the cause – in fact I almost anticipated such a result – I did not try again, but was only too glad to escape from such filth and stench.

The advice and urgent warnings of the villagers at Mani did not deflect him from his determination to cross the difficult and dangerous Manirung Pass. With a team of eighty reluctant and apprehensive porters he eventually reached the top at an elevation of 18 000 feet. His horizon was bounded by innumerable peaks (Plate 18) while far below the Spiti River had diminished to a thin vein of silver in the dark valley. Quickly unpacking his camera, Bourne succeeded in taking three photographs before clouds obscured this impressive panorama.

Traversing high passes, inching his way along narrow mountain paths, Bourne pressed on to the source of the Ganges. His enthusiasm for mountain photography understandably began to wane after two days and nights camped on the exposed face of the Neela Pass, miserably cold and wet, with supplies ominously low. In due course his tenacity and resilience brought him to the ice cave at the foot of the Gangotri glacier, whence rushed forth the waters of the holy Ganges. An attempt to photograph also the source of the Jumna was frustrated by a porter stumbling and breaking his only developing bath. He made a mental note never to travel again without a spare bath in case of similar accidents. After an absence of six months he reached Simla in time for Christmas.

After a short visit to England in 1867, when he married, Bourne returned to photograph other parts of the sub-continent. The *Neilgherry Excelsior,* in welcoming his photographs of Ootacamund, as proof that this hill station in the south was in no way inferior to those in the north, marvelled at the absence of 'stains from dirty chemicals, dirty hands, or careless manipulation, and the most delicate skies and distances show not a trace of those blemishes which so commonly disfigure even good photographs.' Bourne's technical competence was appreciated with equal enthusiasm by the *British Journal of Photography* (11 January 1867).

How travelling through such sultry scenes, oppressed betimes with heat, wind and dust, Mr Bourne has managed to secure such faultless pictures we cannot imagine; for there is not a speck or spot to disfigure them, not a trace of fog, no fracture of the collodion even at the corners, no pinholes, and, in brief, none of those technical shortcomings so commonly met with in the productions of all save a few of our best home artists. . . When we examine some of the temples of white marble, and find the most perfect softness pervading their details, and in the same picture trees and general vegetation, together with figures, water, and other surrounding subjects, all in correct keeping – no effect obtained at the expense or by the sacrifice of any part – we are constrained to admit that the artist is possessed of manipulative or chemical resources shared in common by few.

Samuel Bourne's experiences demonstrate some of the problems met by photographers working in the tropics.

The veteran photographer John McCosh in his *Advice to Officers in India* (1856) rejected the flimsy, folding, portable cameras used in Europe. They would admit light and dust through the cracks caused by shrinkage in high temperatures. Only brass-bound cameras constructed of well-seasoned mahogany or walnut would withstand heat and damp. The Gandolfi firm in south-east London used specially-scented Russian leather for cameras intended for the East, hoping this exotic material would deter insects from eating the bellows. K.B. Oakely, who used some of his photographs in his *Pagoda of Hallibeed* (1859), soon discovered that he had to abandon or modify processes he had used successfully in England. Many papers read at meetings of photographic societies in India recommended innovations or adaptations of existing methods. Mr Fosberg, for instance, urged members of the Photographic Society of Bengal to consider the advantages of using talc instead of fragile glass for making negatives. Some photographers believed that the collodion imported from England needed some additive such as bromide to delay its decomposition. The Chairman of the Photographic Society of Bengal thought that the only way photographers could ensure having fresh supplies of collodion was by preparing their own solutions. Samuel Bourne found that collodion would often start drying before he had finished spreading it over the glass plate, thus reducing its sensitivity. The Deputy Commissioner of Kangra, P.M. Egerton, complained that his collodion 'shrivels up and peels off the plate when drying, though carefully sheltered from the sun and wind; and I am constantly losing some of my best pictures in this way.' G. Henderson, the medical officer on T.D. Forsyth's expedition to Yarkand in 1870, was perturbed to find that above 15 000 feet his collodion started boiling when the stopper was removed from the bottle. Apart from the heat, which exhausted the photographer as well as marring his work, there was every likelihood of dust particles settling on the wet collodion plates, producing unsightly spots on the negatives. Damp could ruin paper stocks and render shutter blinds on cameras sluggish. An unlucky Mr Gray working in Bengal in the 1850s lost a whole year's work through damp affecting his plates. Samuel Bourne learnt to his cost that damp could also cause reticulation of the plate.

The disadvantages of collodion persuaded some photographers like Captain T. Biggs of the Bombay Artillery to stick to the older calotype process. There was of course the inconvenience of the longer exposure time needed with calotypes – anything from four to six minutes for buildings. For calotype photographers the best time of the day to work was reckoned to be early morning before the inevitable breezes got up, causing trees and shrubs to sway and creating blurred images on photographs. The time of day was critical for all photographers whatever process they used. The morning light was best but there was a danger that any fine details might be obscured by long and intense shadows. The glare from the afternoon sun was certain to produce hard black and white prints devoid of any subtlety of tone. A pervasive whiteness is characteristic of some early Indian photographs. Bourne, who was particularly proficient in rendering skies, evoked the admiration of one correspondent to the *British Journal of Photography* (1 October 1869). 'But the thing that struck me most was the clearness and cleanness of the skies. None of them were blacked out [it was a common practice to black out skies on negatives], and all of them without spot or blemish of any kind.'

In assessing the work of early Indian photographers the technical problems these pioneers had to solve should not be forgotten. Let Samuel Bourne have the last word.

To practise photography in England – say on the grassy banks of a stream, the margin of a quiet lake, in the shady avenues of some noble park, or the secluded recesses of some lovely glen with every comfort and convenience at hand – is one thing; to practise it on a journey amid the wilds of the Himalayas, in the extreme of heat or cold, (for it is generally one or the other), when undergoing the fatigue of a long march on foot without roads and subject to every inconvenience, is quite another thing.
British Journal of Photography, 18 February 1870

Taj Mahal at Agra

Plate 1 A popular subject with Indian photographers, in this instance Charles Linkfold: one of two intricately carved stone windows in the fifteenth century mosque built at Ahmadabad by Sidi Saiyid, a former slave of Ahmad Shah, the first king of Gujarat. The delicate stone tracery measures only 10 feet by 7 feet. The distinguished architectural historian James Fergusson praised 'the vegetable forms [which] are conventionalized just to the extent required for the purpose. . . There are some exquisite specimens of tracery in precious marbles at Agra and Delhi, but none quite equal to this'.

8

Plate 2 In the mid-seventeenth century the Mughal Emperor Shah Jahan added the Moti Masjid, the 'Pearl Mosque', to the cluster of exquisite buildings in the Fort at Agra. James Fergusson declared it was 'one of the purest and most elegant buildings of its class to be found anywhere'. Peace and serenity pervade the hall whose pillars are made of marble flecked with delicate veins of white, blue and grey. A contemporary inscription in black mosaic marble poetically proclaims it to be 'an exalted palace of Paradise made of a single resplendent pearl'.

Plate 3 The temple of Rameswaram, where Siva has been worshipped since the twelfth century, stands above a freshwater lake on a sacred island off the south-east coast of India. Its immense size and complexity of corridors make it one of the most memorable monuments in the subcontinent. E.D. Lyon, who took this photograph during the late 1860s, explained 'the difficulty of procuring a good perspective in the long corridors of the temples – one of which exceeds seven hundred feet in length. . . The light in these is very uneven, and the magnesium wire, in consequence of the volume of smoke it produces, could not be employed; so that, in many instances, light had to be turned on by means of natives stationed at certain points with reflectors.'

Plate 4 One of the many courtyards within the massive red sandstone walls of the Fort at Agra. The buildings which the Emperors Akbar, Jahangir and Shah Jahan added, beautifully decorated with inlaid work of floral and abstract designs, rank with the best of Mughal architecture. The photograph was taken by Charles Shepherd and A. Robertson, who began a photographic business in Agra in 1862 (*see p. 3*).

Plate 5 The first European to discover the Jain temples on Mount Abu in Rajputana was James Tod in 1822: 'It was nearly noon when I cleared the pass of Sitla Mata and as the bluff-head of Mount Abu opened upon me, my heart beat with joy as with the sage of Syracuse I exclaimed Eureka.' The temples constructed of white marble brought from quarries nearly thirty miles away, stand on a plateau over 4000 feet above the surrounding desert. Mount Abu is the most sacred place of pilgrimage for Jains, whose craftsmen during the medieval period of Indian history carved the marble columns, doorways and panels into shapes of the most intricate delicacy. This photograph was taken by the firm of Raja Deen Dayal & Sons (*see p. 38*).

Plate 6 Many Hindu temples have temple cars, which are paraded once a year, bearing a statue of the divinity to whom the temple is dedicated, suitably decked with flags, flowers and pictures. This early-nineteenth-century car was photographed in the 1860s at Chamundi in Mysore.

13

Plate 7 The colossal bull representing Nandi, one of the god Siva's attendants, carved from a boulder of granite at the French Rock a few miles from Seringapatam in Mysore.

Plate 8   Robert Gill, here photographed near a temple in West Berar a few years before his death in 1875, was typical of those Englishmen who devoted their lives to Indian studies. He entered the Madras Army in 1842 and two years later was selected to make copies of the famous but fading frescoes in the Buddhist caves at Ajanta. There he spent the rest of his days in inhospitable country and, despite his isolation from fellow Europeans and frequent bouts of fever, produced about thirty full-sized murals for the museum of the East India Company in Leadenhall Street in London.

15

Plate 9 Photographs of the Indian divinities, Sarasvati and Subrahmanya, photographed in the Great Temple at Madura by E.D. Lyon in the late 1860s. Sarasvati, the goddess of learning, features in the iconography of Hindus, Buddhists and Jains. She is usually depicted playing a *vina*, a stringed musical instrument. Subrahmanya or Skanda, the god of war, is an ancient god of the Dravidians in southern India, where many temples are dedicated to him.

Plate 10 A garden gateway, at Khajuraho, 'the city of the Gods', once lost in the encroaching jungle, but rediscovered by the British in 1840. It provides some of the best examples in North India of Hindu architecture and sculpture of the tenth and eleventh centuries. The tall towers of the temples are thickly populated with sensual carvings of gods making love to *apsaras* or nymphs with remarkably supple bodies.

Plate 11 The *makbara* or mausoleum designed for his own use by Sheikh Baha-ud-din Bhar, Minister to the Nawab of Junagadh at Kathiawar in Western India. It is an example of the decline in the quality of Islamic architecture in India at the end of the nineteenth century. Nevertheless, no matter how much its baroque bravura may be disliked, it is a building of some power and originality.

Plate 12 The great fortress of ▷ Gwalior and its palaces stand on a sandstone hill which rises abruptly above the plain to a height of some 300 feet and extends for nearly two miles. From the east it presents an imposing silhouette of towers and fretted domes above the long line of battlements. This photograph shows the principal entrance at the top of a very steep incline.

Bourne 1396

19

Plate 13 A small carriage pulled by deer, a precious conceit belonging to the Maharaja Gaekwar of Baroda, one of the three premier princes of India. He was proud of his collection of exotic transport, which also included gold and silver carriages and carts hauled by bullocks splendidly decked in cloth of gold and covered with gold and silver bells.

Plate 14 The principal street ▷ in Agra, one of a set of thirty views of the town published by J. Hogarth of the Haymarket in London in 1857. The photographer, John Murray, who was Principal of the Medical School at Agra, always used calotypes or paper negatives. Most of the figures sitting beneath the shop awnings are blurred because this process required an exposure of about four to six minutes. The shadows that fall across the street in the original sepia-coloured photograph possess the soft, velvety feel of a drypoint etching.

Plate 15 A photograph of merchant houses on a canal in Srinagar, 1864. It was taken by Samuel Bourne (*see p. 5*), who wrote: 'Some of the views of these narrow canals are very picturesque. They are overhung with four, five and six-storied wooden houses, which are generally built on props and leaning, some one way and some another, spanned in several places with a single-arched stone bridge, dark and hoary, the whole here and there relieved by vines and creepers clinging to the lattices or climbing over the roofs and bridges.' The artist Val Prinsep, who was not so captivated, thought 'the town has a tumble down "has been" sort of look'.

Plate 16 A common sight in the Vale of Kashmir were the poplars lining the roads and they extended for about a mile on one particular stretch of road in Srinagar. Samuel Bourne, attracted by the striking perspective they provided and the repetitive lines of shadows, took this photograph in 1864.

24

Plate 17 A photograph of village life in Bengal taken by Samuel Bourne in the late 1860s. Though the villagers are clearly aware of the camera they seem relaxed and natural in their poses (*see p. 38*).

Plate 18 A photograph taken by Bourne just below the Manirung Pass (*see p. 6*): 'I seemed to stand on a level with the highest of these innumerable peaks, and as the eye wandered seemed as though I stood on a solitary island in the middle of some vast polar ocean, whose rolling waves and billows, crested with foam, had been suddenly seized in their mad career by some omnipotent power and commanded to perpetual rest.'

Plate 19 Until a harbour was constructed in the 1880s at Madras, nervous passengers disembarked cautiously in *massulah* boats, which were specially constructed to enable them to ride the surf that relentlessly pounds the shore in a long line of waves. They were flat-bottomed without a keel, had high sides, and were sewn in pliable sections with coconut fibre to yield to the force of the strong surf. Passengers sat on a bench in the stern of the boat facing the eight to twelve rowers.

Plate 20 Flimsy catamarans accompanied the *massulah* boats to rescue any unfortunate passengers who might be swept overboard. These primitive craft consisted of three logs, about 20 to 25 feet long, lashed together. Two or three men handled them with remarkable dexterity. 'Some of these [men] brought letters from shore, well secured from the sea, in the conical caps of the bearers,' wrote one passenger, a Mrs Sherwood, 'for, as we found afterwards, these catamaran people are forced, owing to the violence of the surf, to dive under the first three waves after leaving the shore.'

Plate 21 An English-style garden in the grounds of Makarpura Palace, Baroda, with a charming trellis-work summerhouse, clearly inspired by Victorian glass conservatories. Determined and dedicated English garden lovers imported seeds and horticultural practices from home and the Royal Botanic Gardens at Kew provided a nucleus of trained gardeners who found employment in botanic gardens, municipal parks and the estates of Indian princes, who were only too ready to abandon their traditional gardens.

Plate 22 The South American water-lily, *Victoria amazonica*, flourishing in a park in Udaipur. Its large leaves are reputed to be able to sustain the weight of a child but it is more than likely that in this photograph the child in the chair was supported by some judicious underpinning beneath the leaf. The British were instrumental in introducing many foreign plants, both economic and ornamental, into cultivation in India.

Plate 23 A view of one of the palm-fringed beaches in Ceylon taken by Scowen and Company, the leading firm of photographers in the 1880s. The outrigger canoes, which were built to withstand the roughest seas, are still used by the island's fishermen.

Plate 24 A corner of a *kioung* or monastery in Amarapura, the capital of Burma until 1859. The craftsmanship in these buildings, usually constructed of teak, evoked the admiration of Henry Yule when he visited the country with a British mission in 1855: 'It is impossible to look at these kioungs without a feeling of wonder how a people so deficient in all domestic appliances could be capable of designing and executing such exquisite workmanship.' The photograph is one of a series published by Captain Linnaeus Tripe of the 12th Regiment Native Infantry, who was the mission's official photographer.

Plate 25 Bubonic plague spread across China during the 1890s, reaching Bombay from Hongkong in 1896. Many people died and cremation centres similar to the one shown in this photograph were established all over the city. In an attempt to check the epidemic, the Chief Plague Officer, W.C. Rand, was forced to use harsh measures, which the public strongly resented and which provoked anti-government agitation. Rand and his assistant, Lieutenant Ayerst, were assassinated in Poona in June 1897.

Plate 26 The burning ghats at Benares, the sacred city of Hinduism, with a body being purified in the holy waters of the Ganges before cremation. 'On landing at this wharf one is half suffocated by the dense foetid smoke which hangs over it like a bluish dome,' wrote the traveller Louis Rousselet (1878). 'On all sides the funeral piles send up their long flames, and their cracklings are accompanied by sinister sounds. The workmen of this dismal place, with their bodies naked and blackened by the soot, like real demons, stir the fires by means of long bars of iron, or throw jars of oil upon them.'

Plate 27 The Sanskrit word 'sati,' meaning 'virtuous one', was applied to the widow who joined her late husband on his funeral pyre. The Mughals tried to discourage the practice, which was prohibited by the British in 1829-30. Poignant memorial stones such as those shown in this photograph of the 1870s are to be found all over India. 'Each luckless woman', according to General C. Hervey (1892), 'was required, by way of sealing her "determination" to immolate herself, to place the palm of her right hand upon some yellow daub presented to her in a platter as she passed out, and to press it against the wall of the gateway, the hand-mark thus left being subsequently cut out in the wall, or, as in some instances, a hand was fashioned in marble from the model afforded by the impression and fixed upon it.'

Princes and Peasants

The Indian sub-continent, as large as all the countries of Europe, is inhabited by people speaking as many different languages. Where it probably outstrips Europe is in its ethnic diversity. Within the broad classification of tall, fair Aryans in the north, stocky, dark-skinned Dravidians in the south, and mixed Aryo-Dravidians in the central regions, the racial permutations seem infinite. This bewildering complexity of peoples and their cultures made an immediate impact on Europeans. Emily Eden, the sister of the Governor-General, Lord Auckland, persuaded rulers and their servants, farmers and fakirs and even traders from Tibet to pose for her. A selection of her drawings was lithographed in *Portraits of the Princes and Peoples of India*, which was published in London in 1844. Ethnology became a fashionable area of research. The Schlagintweit brothers, who swept through Central and Northern India in the 1850s, avidly collecting specimens of practically everything they saw, took plaster casts of faces, hands and feet. Their unfortunate victims submitted meekly, their faces smeared with oil or clarified butter to facilitate the removal of the plaster and with paper cornets stuffed up their nostrils to let them breathe.

Probably the earliest Indian ethnographic work to make use of photographs was William Johnson's *Oriental Races and Tribes: Residents and Visitors of Bombay* (London, 1863). Johnson, an official in the Bombay Civil Service, photographed groups of people in his studio against a scenic backdrop. Sixty-one photographs were pasted in the book which the author said 'was made with great labour and in many instances with no little persuasion addressed to the scrupulous personages, whose effigies have been successfully delineated by the solar ray.'

In December 1861 the following directive was issued by the Government of India:

> Each Local Government is expected to collect into one collection such photographic likenesses of the races and classes within its borders as it may obtain and furnish a very brief notice of each. The likenesses are to be sent to the Central Committee of the London Exhibition in Calcutta.

From these photographs a selection was made and displayed to the crowds that wandered through the 1862 International Exhibition in London. One of the photographers engaged in this project was Dr B. Simpson of the Indian Medical Service, who was afterwards commissioned by the Government of Bengal to photograph its native peoples. His prints, together with those of

Men of the Nicobar Islands

other photographers (including Tosco Peppé, who 'brought his camera to bear on some of the most primitive of human beings, the Juangs, never previously subjected to the process'), were skilfully reinterpreted by lithography for publication in E.T. Dalton's *Descriptive Ethnology of Bengal* (Calcutta, 1872).

The Todas, a primitive tribe living in the Nilgiris in South India, aroused the interest of Lieutenant-Colonel William Marshall of the Bengal Staff Corps. His book, *A Phrenologist amongst the Todas* (London, 1873), investigated with scientific thoroughness their culture, discreetly censored for women readers, and described in precise detail their physiological characteristics. He noted for instance that men's bodies, after passing through a downy period, were carpeted with hair by the time they were thirty and that women often had fine hairs between their shoulder blades. And with just a hint of envy he recorded that 'a paunch is never to be seen.'

A similar sort of investigation was carried out by M.V. Portman, Extra Assistant Superintendent at Port Blair in the Andaman Islands. Fearing that the islanders were in danger of becoming extinct, he offered to undertake a photographic study of them 'in all the actions of their lives' for the British Museum. He was convinced of the sociological value of such surveys.

> Details of the lives of the savage border tribes such as the Nagas, etc., the musical instruments of India, showing how they are held and played; the Indian artisan at work and for lady photographers who can gain access thereto, zenana interiors and the lives of native women are all subjects which would repay the taking.
> *Journal of the Photographic Society of India* July, 1891, 116

The British Museum, which had already received a collection of Andamanese artefacts from him, readily agreed and Portman was busy during the 1890s photographing the islanders in formal poses at their various occupations (Plate 43). At the same time W. Molesworth recorded exact body measurements of fifty representative males in the North Andamans.

In the late 1850s, Lord Canning, Governor-General and the first Viceroy of India, and his wife decided to compile a photographic record of the country and its people to take back with them to England. Army officers and civilians were encouraged to make good use of their cameras on their travels and to deposit prints with the Cannings. Captain Melville Clarke of the 1st Light Cavalry used some of the photographs he took on his journey through northern India in his *From Simla through Ladac and Cashmere* (Calcutta, 1862). P.H. Egerton's *Journal of a Tour through Spiti to the Frontier of Chinese Tibet* (London, 1864) included photographs of monks, merchants and peasants. With photographs coming from all quarters Lord and Lady Canning soon acquired more than they needed for their personal albums. What originally began as an informal request from the Governor-General was now put on an official basis, although no overall policy as to the type of photographs to

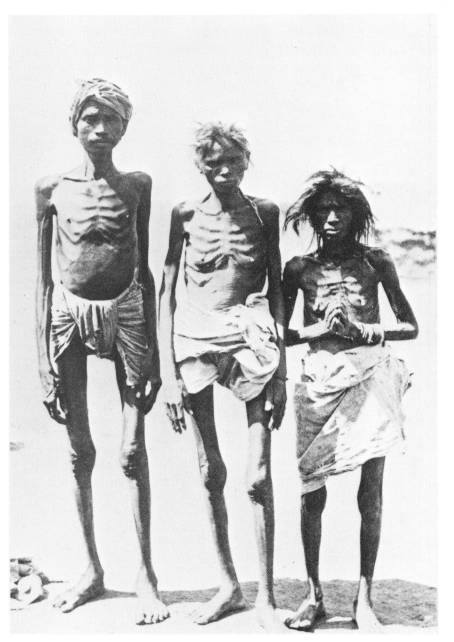

Victims of a famine

be collected was imposed. Copies of the photographs, which included portraits and groups of people, were sent to the India Office in London, where John Forbes Watson added them to the collections in the India Museum, of which he was Director.

In 1863 John William Kaye, Secretary of the Political and Secret Department at the India Office, received from the Government of India a series of photographs of the peoples of East Bengal (Plate 39). Impressed by the remarkable quality of these portraits, the India Office agreed to pay for their mounting together with printed captions. A few months later Kaye discovered that Forbes Watson also had a collection of photographs of Indian ethnic groups. Both men agreed it would be a highly desirable project to publish a selection of them and recommended the issuing of eighteen sets, each containing about eight hundred photographs with descriptive text. After several modifications to this original proposal, the India Office published in eight volumes between 1868 and 1875 *The People of India: A Series of Photographic Illustrations, with Descriptive Letterpress, of the Races and Tribes of Hindustan.* Two hundred sets, half for official use, were printed of what must be the first major ethnographical work to make extensive use of photographs. Altogether four hundred and sixty-eight photographs were pasted in each set, representing the work of more than fifteen photographers, including such distinguished practitioners as W.W. Hooper, Shepherd & Robertson, B. Simpson and J. Waterhouse.

By the late 1870s photography was no longer a novelty; commercial studios proliferated in all the major cities, and as conclusive evidence of its popularity the Photographic Society of India was formed in 1886. Ladies who would formerly have painted vignettes of Indian life now resorted to the camera. Lady Dufferin, the wife of the Viceroy, during her apprentice days as a photographer confided to her journal that she 'felt extremely nervous over it.' But at the same time she recorded the irritation she and her husband felt at the intrusion of the camera, 'for we never move anywhere that we don't see a photographer pointing at us from the top of a carriage, or from some unexpected vantage point.'

Most Indian princes succumbed sooner or later to the attractions of this new pastime. The artist, Val Prinsep, who was commissioned by the Government of India to paint a picture of the Imperial Assemblage of India for presentation to Queen Victoria when she became Empress of India, spent 1877 travelling around India painting the portraits of princes. His *Glimpses of Imperial India* (London, 1878) makes frequent mention of the princely passion for photography. The Maharaja of Jaipur devoted much of his leisure to photography while the Maharaja of Dhar had himself photographed 'in every conceivable position. He sent for our amusement eight large books, in which, without exaggeration, there were fifty photographs of himself.' The wealth and power of these Indian princes is vividly

Maharaja Raghuraj Singh of Rewah

encapsulated in these portraits. Flanked by attentive ministers and courtiers, they complacently pose secure in the knowledge of their undisputed authority; or perhaps seated as a single figure, one hand negligently resting on an adjacent table, the other holding a ceremonial sword which sweeps across the photograph in an elegant diagonal line. King Thibaw of Burma at one time had a Frenchman as his Court photographer (Plate 45). The poor man, however, found the appointment nerve-racking. Never certain whether the royal reaction to one of his photographs, especially if it happened to be one of Queen Supayalat, would be a handful of rubies or the threat of decapitation, he prudently abandoned his precarious position.

One of the most successful Indian portrait photographers was Lala Deen Dayal (Plate 28). Originally trained as a draughtsman, he took up photography and when the Prince of Wales graciously posed for him during his visit to India in 1875 his professional reputation was established. After that stroke of good fortune, commissions came in thick and fast. He photographed native chiefs when he accompanied Sir Henry Daly on his tour of Bundelkhand. His appointment as photographer to the Viceroy was soon followed by that of Court photographer to the Nizam of Hyderabad.

Orthodox Indian ladies who still observed the seclusion forced on them by purdah were reluctant to be photographed by men, especially strangers. They allowed themselves to be photographed by women but framed photographs were discreetly veiled to conceal them from prying eyes. In 1892 Deen Dayal proudly announced the establishment of a 'Zenana Photographic Studio' in Hyderabad under the respectable superintendence of Mrs Leverick, the wife of one of the editors of the *Deccan Times*. Behind high walls every precaution was taken in this purdah studio to protect 'high-born native ladies' from 'the gaze of the profane and stern.'

Some of these early photographic portraits of people instantly communicate their subjects' diffidence; they peer anxiously at the camera, desperately serious, never smiling, amid pieces of furniture carefully positioned about them like so many stage props. This shyness gave way to apprehension among superstitious villagers, who feared that being photographed would in some way shorten their lives. This instinctive unease made it extremely difficult for photographers to get natural poses. A 'Bombay Amateur' expressed his frustration in a letter to the *British Journal of Photography* (1 August 1862):

> Only point a camera at a native, and notwithstanding his natural grace, suppleness of limb, and easy carriage and bearing when taken unawares, from fear of being shot, or converted into some uncouth animal by means of necromancy, he becomes on seeing you as *rigid* as the camera-stand, or moves away altogether or neither moves nor stays. All the posturing and explaining and reasoning and coaxing or offers of money you can bestow upon him in the course of an hour or two will not induce him to *unbend*.

Samuel Bourne, who did not readily accept defeat, also despaired of getting his subjects to relax:

> The only difficulty I had generally to contend with was the obstinacy of the natives when I wanted to introduce them into my pictures. By no amount of talking and acting could I get them to stand or sit in an easy, natural attitude. Their idea of giving life to a picture was to stand bolt upright, with their arms down as stiff as pokers, their chins turned up as if they were standing to have their throats cut.
> *British Photographic Journal* 25 June 1867

Val Prinsep noticed regretfully that Delhi artists were now employing photographs to execute their fastidious miniature portraits. The outlines of a photograph would be carefully traced on ivory and then dexterously coloured. Photographs themselves would sometimes be heavily over-painted in water-colours and gold leaf to simulate original drawings. The camera was insidiously influencing, if not replacing, traditional artistic skills.

Plate 28 The Maharaja Bhan Pratab Singh of Bijawar and his court. He succeeded to the throne in 1847 at the age of five and ruled until his death in 1899. For his services to the British during the Mutiny he received a *khilat* (a ceremonial present) and an hereditary salute of eleven guns. Photograph by Deen Dayal.

40

Plate 31 Polo, an ancient game much liked by the Mughals, survived in a primitive form in India until the first polo club was formed by the British in Assam in 1859. This photograph shows polo players in Manipur, where, as R. Pemberton, writing in 1835, explained, 'the national game of Hockey, which is played by every male of the country capable of sitting a horse, renders them all expert equestrians; and it was by men and horses so trained, that the princes of Muneepoor [Manipur] were able for many years not only to repel the aggressions of the Burmahs, but to save the whole country'.

Plate 32 The British in eighteenth-century India apparently enjoyed watching a nautch or dance which was usually arranged for them by their Indian hosts. But a certain Mrs Sherwood was alarmed by 'the influence of these Nautch girls over the other sex, even over men who have been bred up in England, and who have known, admired and respected their own countrywomen.' By Victorian times enchantment had turned to indifference and even disgust. 'You Europeans are apt to picture to yourselves a Nach as a most attractive spectacle,' wrote T.D. Broughton in 1892, 'but once witnessed it generally dissolves the illusion.'

3087 — EMBROIDERERS

44

Plate 33 Embroidery in India has close links with folk art and its skills are handed down from generation to generation.

Plate 34 Hindu priests engaged in writing religious texts. The rectangular shape of the page derives from the palm leaf, which was a common writing material in South and South-East Asia.

Plate 35 A Marathi barber and customer, still a familiar sight on the streets of India.

Plate 36 Burmese snake charmers with a hamadryad. Snake charmers employed various methods of rendering the reptiles harmless; breaking off the poison teeth was the commonest; another was to cut into the poison sac from beneath the lip on each side to produce a fistula which would prevent the snake from delivering a poisonous bite.

Plate 37 A photograph from Kaye and Watson's *The People of India (see p. 37)* of the Bhurs in Oudh. According to Lt.-Col. William H. Sleeman, writing in *Journey Through The Kingdom of Oude in 1849-50* (1858), 'The Bhurs must have formed town and village communities in Oude at a very remote period, and must have been a civilized people, though they have not left a name, date or legend, inscribed on any monument. Brick ruins of forts, houses and wells are the only relics left of them. Some few of the caste still exist among the lower grades of society as cultivators, police officers, etc. in Oude and other districts north of the Ganges.'

Plate 38 A group of *ghatis* from the agricultural class of the Marathas. They used to work as labourers in Bombay, returning to their villages to farm when they had made sufficient money. This photograph appeared in Johnson and Henderson's *Indian Amateurs' Photographic Album,* which was launched in 1857 as a monthly periodical with three large photographs in each issue.

Plate 39 Two portraits from a collection of photographs of the peoples of East Bengal received by the India Office in London during the early 1860s (*see p. 37*).

50

Plate 40 In 1873 Sir George Campbell, Lieutentant-Governor of Bengal, made an official tour of the eastern borders handing out 'trays of fat puppies as the most acceptable ceremonial present' to local chiefs. He is here photographed with the Raja of Sikkim and later in retirement he recollected the occasion: 'I had a very interesting Durbar to receive the Sikkim Rajah, his family, and following. The ladies are very prominent on these occasions – they have no false modesty as in India. I have still a very successful photograph of that Durbar scene in which, the Rajah being a minor, a robust and comely sister did the honours on his side.'

Plate 41 A photograph of Tibetan nuns at the Ta-Tshang convent in Sikkim, taken by Hoffman during a tour in 1902 by the British Political Officer, Claude White, who described them as 'grossly ignorant . . . but good-natured.' They spent their lives either in the convent or in wandering the countryside seeking alms. On the completion of their novitiate their heads were either shaved or the hair cut very short. Out of doors they wore extraordinary wigs made of brightly-coloured red or yellow wool.

Plate 42 Members of the Toda tribe standing outside their distinctive, half-barrel-shaped, windowless houses. They live in the Nilgiri Hills in South India, where they graze buffaloes and cattle but their principal source of income comes from tourists from nearby Ootacamund (*see p. 79*).

54

Plate 43 The French photographer Oscar Mallitte took the earliest known photographs of Andamanese islanders in December 1857. M.V. Portman also photographed them for the British Museum in the 1890s (*see p. 36*) and two of his studies are reproduced here: (a) a woman of about forty-two of the Puchik-war tribe; (b) a girl of six of the Ta-Yeri tribe. Portman adopted the measured screen devised by J.H. Lamprey, Assistant Secretary of the Royal Geographical Society. 'For Andamanese single figures for scientific measurement, I use a background of canvas lightly stretched, and painted in black and white chequers, each chequer being exactly two inches square.'

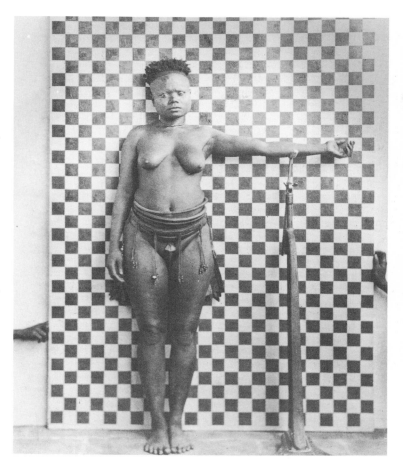

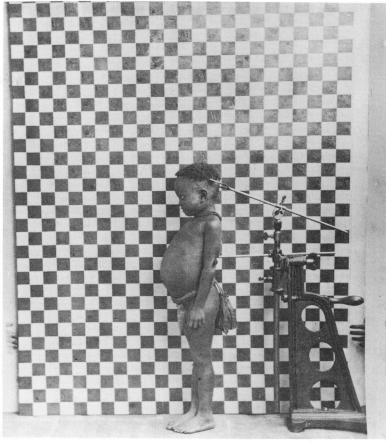

Plate 44 A ceremonial dance of natives of either the Andaman or Nicobar Islands. The original Andamanese and their primitive culture have practically become extinct.

Plate 45 A photograph of King Thibaw, Queen Supayalat and her sister that was found in the Palace at Mandalay by British forces during the Burmese War of 1885. Queen Supayalat, a violent and passionate person, completely dominated her weak husband. Both were exiled to India and, after Thibaw's death in 1916, Supayalat, now a pathetic old woman, was allowed to return to Burma, where she lived quietly in a small house in Rangoon.

Plate 46 An upper-class Burmese family about 1886. The common age for Burmese girls to marry was thirteen or fourteen and for boys eighteen or nineteen. Burmese women were allowed to keep separate any money or possessions they brought to a marriage and to retain them if there was a divorce. A Burmese author writing in 1892 claimed that married women in his country enjoyed greater independence than European women. A Burmese woman had grounds for divorce if her husband was unable or refused to support her, was constantly ill or became a cripple.

Plate 47 A young Burmese woman and servants standing near a well.

Plate 48 A Burmese woman with a cheroot. Everyone – men, women and children – smoked in Burma and the women were proud of their skill in rolling cheroots. Indeed, a woman's accomplishments were considered imperfect until she could make cheroots perfectly. These varied in length from about six to eight inches and were about one inch in diameter at one end, tapering to half an inch at the other. They consisted of chopped tobacco leaves, mixed with small pieces of pitch, rolled in the leaf of the teak.

Plate 49 Burmese girls grooming their hair. Both men and women took great pride in the length of their hair, which could reach below the knees. The hair was washed daily in rice or coconut water to encourage it to grow. The men tied their hair in a knot on the top of the head while the women wore theirs on the back.

61

Plate 50 Burmese convicts on a treadmill in 1901.

Campaigns and Conquests

At the beginning of Queen Victoria's reign the East India Company, although its powers had been drastically curtailed by successive British Governments, still maintained an army which at the time of the Mutiny numbered nearly a quarter of a million men, only nineteen per cent of whom were Europeans. It was really three distinct armies based upon the Presidencies of Bengal, Bombay and Madras. They were reinforced by regiments of the British Army, which had been stationed in India since the late eighteenth century. The effectiveness of the Indian Army as a fighting force was impaired by the retention of superannuated officers, slack discipline and problems of caste amongst Indian soldiers. The Governor-General, Lord William Bentinck, just before his departure from India in 1835, pronounced 'the Indian Army to be the least efficient and the most expensive in the world.' Its efficiency and reliability were severely tested in 1857-8 when regiments of Indian troops rebelled. Fortunately for the British the Mutiny did not spread; Sikh and Punjabi troops remained loyal. This near disaster meant the end of Company rule and the direct imposition of the British Crown. The Indian Army was reorganized: it was not allowed to have any artillery; a British Army battallion was attached to every Indian brigade as a constant watchdog and the ratio of British to Indian troops was roughly one to two. Towards the end of Victoria's reign about a third of the British Army was normally stationed in India, policing the sub-continent and campaigning with great gusto on the North-West Frontier.

For much of the time this huge force remained in cantonments or military stations, indulging in long route marches of up to 500 miles, which some declared in comfortable retrospect to have been the great experience of their soldiering. As the civil lines and local villages with their dubious amenities were out of bounds to troops, the cantonments were largely self-contained. Other ranks, who were preponderantly Irish, lived rather austerely in brick barracks, where they were confined for their own well-being when temperatures soared. For a few rupees a week they could employ a dhoby to wash their clothes and a bobachee to cook their stodgy food.

An officer, on the other hand, lived exceedingly well: billiards in the mess, cricket on the parched grass, and horse-racing and hunting in the neighbourhood. He even campaigned in comfort, with servants, wine, a portable bath and his twelve-bore rifle just in case the opportunity for some sport occurred. A young ensign's daily routine in 1855 was perhaps not untypical.

He rose at 04.30 hours to parade for an hour in the cool of early morning; then to the officers' mess for coffee before returning to his billet for a bath and breakfast; private drill or some other suitable occupation in his quarters lasted until tiffin at 14.00 hours; at 17.30 hours he could be found relaxing in the park before dining in the mess at 19.30 hours; cards or billiards followed; at 22.00 hours he was exhausted and ready for bed.

For much of the last century the main preoccupation of the British was the defence of India against Russian encroachment. Mountainous, inhospitable Afghanistan stood between the two great powers and its continuance as an independent neutral state was vital to British strategy. It was this fear of

British spy caught and mutilated by the forces of Nana Sahib

Russian ambitions that panicked Lord Auckland into forming the Army of the Indus, which invaded Afghanistan in 1839. The ruler, Dost Muhammad, fled and Shah Shuja, the British candidate, was placed on the empty throne in Kabul. The Afghans rebelled, the British command bickered and quarrelled, essential stores were lost and ignominious retreat was the only alternative to starvation. Thus, in January 1842, the army began its disastrous withdrawal ending in the annihilation of the British forces; only one survivor got through the Khyber to reveal the fate of 16000 men. So ended the First Afghan War, but the Great Game, as this rivalry between Britain and Russia was flippantly called, erupted again in the Second Afghan War in 1878. When, in the following year, the British envoy and his escort were massacred in Kabul, British troops under General Roberts reoccupied the Afghan capital. The skirmishes with the fierce and predatory tribes of the North-West Frontier region – the Afridis, the Mohmands, the Orakzais and the Wazirs – became legendary and were the stuff of which Victorian schoolboy adventure stories were made. The relief of the British Resident besieged in a fort in the small mountain state of Chitral in 1895 aroused the admiration of the nation. Two years later, when a massive military operation was mounted against the Afridis and Orakzais in the Tirah Valley, public imagination was captured by the storming of the Dargai Pass by the Gordon Highlanders, urged on by a wounded piper who, supporting himself against a boulder, went on gallantly playing.

The first photographs taken during any military campaign are generally believed to be the few daguerreotypes made in the course of the Mexican War of 1846-8. Second place probably belongs to the photographs of John McCosh, who accompanied the East India Company's forces during the Second Sikh War in 1848-9. Since he used the slow calotype process he was not able to take any photographs of troops in action and contented himself with portraits of officers of the 2nd Brigade and its commanders, Lord Gough and Sir Charles Napier. McCosh, who will be remembered as the earliest war photographer in Asia, joined the 5th Battery Bengal Artillery, which fought in the Second Burmese War of 1852-3. There he photographed on prints measuring 20.5 by 21 inches the palaces, pagodas and monasteries of Rangoon and Prome, with glimpses of troops, their equipment and captured Burmese guns. This campaign ended with the British annexation of Lower Burma but sporadic fighting continued until the Third and final Burmese War some thirty years later.

The rebellion of the sepoys in the Indian Army which led to the massacre of British men, women and children at Cawnpore and the siege of Delhi and Lucknow focused the attention of all western nations on India. The photographer James Robertson, who had been photographing views and camp life during the Crimean War, and his brother-in-law, Felice Beato, hastened to India in search of spectacular subjects. Beato arrived in February 1858, just a month before the final relief of Lucknow. He photographed with a clinical precision the ruins of the Residency and the carnage at Sikandarbagh, a walled garden where about 2000 trapped sepoys had been slaughtered the previous November. As late as March the following year one eye-witness was repelled by the 'quantities of human hair and bones still lying about, and the smell, even now, was intolerable.' The remains had been buried by the time Beato arrived but he was not going to be denied the authentic touch for which his photographs are renowned (Plate 52). According to the memoirs of Sir George Campbell, the Judicial Commissioner at Lucknow, 'The great pile of bodies had been decently covered before the photographer [i.e. Beato] could take them, but he insisted on having them uncovered to be photographed before they were finally disposed of.'

After the relief of Lucknow a number of albums of photographs of former British residents were discovered in the ruins of the buildings and were quickly sold at extremely high prices. Captain Trevor Wheler acquired one of them and gave it to W.H. Russell, *The Times* war correspondent. At some

Three little girls at Lucknow

subsequent stage the album was split, one part being presented by Russell's daughter to the India Office Library in 1922. By a stroke of singular good fortune the India Office Library was able to purchase the missing part in 1975. It is a poignant record. A number of the men, women and children in the salt print portraits lost their lives in the siege. The photographer was an Indian, Ahmad Ali Khan, whose services, as the only photographer in Lucknow in 1856, had been eagerly sought. The Chaplain of the Residency, the Rev. Henry Polehampton, grumbled at the time that Ali Khan was 'getting bumptious through having so much notice taken of him.' Regardless of the fact that he had commanded a company of rebel sepoys during the Mutiny, he received a pardon and even obtained a renewal of the pension awarded him by the former King of Oudh.

Beato was by no means the only photographer to record the devastation caused during the Mutiny. Dr John Murray, Principal of the Medical School at Agra, produced well-composed prints of Delhi and Cawnpore. Another medical man, Surgeon Major P.G. Fitzgerald of the 27th Madras Native Infantry, also found time to photograph the aftermath of these historic events. After receiving tuition from both Beato and Murray, Major R.C. Tytler of the 38th Native Infantry took five hundred large calotypes, mainly of places connected with the Mutiny.

The issue of photographic equipment was now becoming a regular practice. In 1858 the Military Department 'sanctioned the construction at

Villagers crucified by Burmese dacoits

public expense of a doolie [a litter] by Major N.O. Lennox for the conveyance of the photographic apparatus required for use in the field, and the employment of six Bearers to carry the doolie in question.' Officers were now campaigning with cameras at the ready. Lieutenant H. Senior of the 2nd Gurkhas found time to photograph incidents during the Ambeyla expedition which set out in 1863 to suppress a highly organized band of native fanatics operating in the inaccessible Mahabun Mountains in the troublesome Frontier region.

At the time of the Second Afghan War the Army asked J. Burke, a professional photographer of Murree and Rawalpindi, to join the Peshawar Valley Field Forces as 'photographic artist'. Burke stipulated terms of engagement similar to those he had previously negotiated with the Army; namely, 1000 rupees a month with local honorary rank, and free transport and rations for himself and his servants. In return he would provide all photographic equipment and chemicals and six copies of every photograph he took, with the option of purchasing additional copies at a specified rate. Never anticipating that these terms would be rejected by the Government, Burke rashly attached himself to the division invading Afghanistan. When he learnt that his conditions were not acceptable he returned to India but not before he had taken some remarkably fine photographs of the war, the peace talks with Amir Yakub Khan and the signing of the treaty at Gandamak (Plate 54).

A passion for photography almost brought Colonel W.W. Hooper's military career to an abrupt and disastrous conclusion. No subject was ever too trivial or distateful for his keen eye: officers at leisure, servants at work, a sepoy running amok or starving peasants in the Madras famine of 1876-8 were all meticulously photographed. He was Provost Marshal with the British Expeditionary Force, under the command of General Prendergast, which occupied Upper Burma in 1885. King Thibaw was swiftly deposed and the annexation of his kingdom completed the gradual absorption of the entire Burmese Empire by the British over a period of some sixty years. One of the newspapermen who reported the fall of Mandalay was E.K. Moylan, the Rangoon correspondent of *The Times*. His despatch, which appeared in *The Times* for 5 December 1885, blamed the incompetence of the British command for the outbreak of violence and looting in the city. Furious, General Prendergast had him summarily deported but through the intervention of Lord Randolph Churchill a vengeful Moylan returned to Mandalay determined to discredit Prendergast and his officers. The despatches that followed reveal his vindictiveness and one of them, which *The Times* printed on 21 January 1886, reported that

the Provost Marshal [W.W. Hooper], who is an ardent amateur photographer, is desirous of securing views [of the execution of Burmese] at the precise moment when they are struck by the bullets. To secure this result, after the

65

orders 'Ready' 'Present' have been given to the firing party, the Provost Marshal fixes his camera on the prisoners, who at times are kept waiting for some minutes in that position. The officer commanding the firing party is then directed by the Provost Marshal to give the order to fire at the precise moment when he exposes his plate. So far no satisfactory negative has been obtained, and the experiments are likely to be continued. These proceedings take place before a crowd of mixed nationalities, and cannot fail to have a demoralizing effect on both soldiers and spectators.

Moylan's deliberate insinuation that such inhuman acts (Plate 56) were a common occurrence provoked a storm of protest from home. Indignant Members of Parliament urged that the Provost Marshal be prosecuted, the Viceroy added his condemnation and, of course, Moylan demanded 'a full and impartial inquiry.' Following a court of enquiry at Mandalay in March 1886 Colonel Hooper was publicly reprimanded and one wonders whether he recalled with any resentment the fact that there had been no murmur of public outrage when Felice Beato had photographed the hanging of two rebels after the Mutiny, first coolly steadying the swinging bodies before standing back to photograph them.

Plate 51 Ammunition neatly stacked at Fort William, Calcutta. The rebuilding of the original fort of 1697 was begun in 1757 when Robert Clive was Governor of Bengal. Most of it was completed by 1773 and it still stands on the banks of the River Hooghly, a masterpiece of military engineering, though no gun was ever fired from its battlements. Frederick Fiebig, who took this calotype photograph in the early 1850s, was an artist who used the camera to produce some splendid views of India, which he susbsequently hand-tinted.

Plate 52 Felice Beato's photograph of the interior of the Sikanderbagh, taken some months after it had been stormed by British troops (*see p. 64*). Nearly 2000 rebel sepoys were killed during this action in November 1857. 'There they lay in a heap as high as my head,' wrote Lord Roberts, 'a heaving, surging mass of dead and dying inextricably entangled. It was a sickening sight, one of those which even in the excitement of battle and the flush of victory, make one feel strongly what a horrible side there is to war.'

Plate 53 Officers and men of the 19th Bengal Lancers. This regiment was raised at Cawnpore in 1860 by Lieutenant Fane, mainly from volunteers from Hodson's Horse, and was originally designated Fane's Horse. Its four squadrons included Punjabi Muslims, Sikhs, Dogras and Pathans. It fought in the Second China and Afghan Wars and at the outbreak of the Second World War was the last regiment of horsed cavalry.

Plate 54 Troops of the Peshawar Valley Field Force camped near the fort at Ali Masjid during the Second Afghan War of 1878-9. Photographed by J. Burke (*see p. 65*). Ali Masjid, five miles into the Khyber Pass, controlled access through the Pass from its commanding position on an isolated rock. It was captured by troops of the First Division of the Field Force under General Sir Samuel Browne. During the Tirah campaign in 1897, Afridi tribesmen occupied the fort and burnt it to the ground.

Plate 55 Of all the tribes in the North West Frontier Region, the Afridis and the Waziris were considered the most difficult to pacify. The Afridis were tall, agile mountain men who seemed to be constantly engaged in blood feuds. British troops first encountered them during the Afghan War of 1839-42 and repeated military campaigns in the years that followed never really subdued them (*see p. 64*). They were deadly marksmen with the long-barrelled musket or *jezail*. This carefully posed photograph was taken by Charles Shepherd.

70

Shephend 1387.

71

Plate 56 The execution of dacoits in Burma, photographed by W.W. Hooper (*see p. 65*). After the annexation of the country, bands of these robbers terrorized the population.

Plate 57 The Second Battalion ▷ of the Devonshire Regiment in action against dacoits while they were stationed in Burma in 1890-2. The crucifixion of criminals by the Burmese authorities and of victims by the dacoits was a common form of execution before the Third Burmese War. A photograph of a crucified man, horribly mutilated, appeared in the *Indian Daily News* with an editorial comment that such atrocities would justify the occupation of Burma.

Plate 58 Chitral was an independent state in the Frontier region, ruled by a Mehtar under the supervision of the British Agent at Gilgit. On the death of the Mehtar in 1894, his two sons, Nizam and Amir-ul-Mulk, disputed the succession. The British recognized the elder son, Nizam, who was shot by his brother in January 1895. Amir-ul-Mulk then sought the help of Umra Khan, Chief of Jandol, and attacked Chitral. A British force of about 400 men was raised and Amir-ul-Mulk was captured in February. This photograph shows him with his captors.

Plate 59 The Tirah Field Force ▷ of 35 000 men and 20 000 camp followers was assembled to deal once and for all with the constant skirmishing by the Afridi and Orakzai tribes on the Peshawar and Kohat borders. This photograph shows a field battery at Peshawar before the force invaded Tirah, the summer home of the tribesmen, in 1897. By the early years of the twentieth century, elephants, which had been used to haul heavy artillery, were replaced by draught horses, which were more reliable under fire. Elephants, however, were still used to carry lighter loads of ordnance.

Plate 60 On 12 September 1897 several thousand Orakzai tribesmen overwhelmed the small fort at Saragarhi on the crest of the Samana range in Kohat, killing all the twenty-one men of the 36th Sikhs who defended it. The nearby garrisons of Forts Lockhart and Gulistan had to look on without being able to offer any assistance. The tribesmen then turned their attention to Fort Gulistan, commanded by Major Des Voeux, who had with him his wife, children and a nurse. A quarter of his garrison strength of 165 men was killed or wounded before his besieged fort was relieved by troops under General Yeatman Biggs. This photograph of Mrs Des Voeux and her family, looking remarkably composed, was taken during the siege.

Sahibs and Memsahibs

It was not uncommon for the heavy and unwieldy East Indiamen to take as long as six months (allowing for leisurely stops at Madeira, St Helena and the Cape) to reach India. By the time of Victoria's accession the distance and the time had been shortened by the more direct route through the Mediterranean to Alexandria. Before the canal was opened in 1869 passengers re-embarked at Suez for the final stage of the voyage to India. Landing within the protection of Bombay's natural harbour was a routine affair, but passengers disembarking at Madras had to endure the hazards of being carried to shore through the heavy surf in flimsy *massulah* boats (Plate 19). A much more agreeable approach to India was assured for passengers destined for Calcutta. As the ship moved slowly up the Hooghly River, carefully navigating through its many mudbanks and shoals, the newcomer had time to admire the pleasant prospect of large, white houses with graceful porticoes and verandahs standing in landscaped grounds along the river bank.

He would also notice that everywhere large, green Venetian blinds were firmly fixed over the windows in an attempt to keep rooms cool. And before too long he would ignore the monotonous clicking of punkahs and the splash and dripping of water against the tatties in every European home. The punkah, a large cloth fan suspended from the ceiling and operated by a servant known as a punkah-wallah, surprisingly still survives in remote areas of India. Tatties were screens made of dried grass hung across open doors and the verandah and were kept constantly wet by servants in an attempt to cool the air entering the house.

The commonest form of dwelling was the single-storeyed bungalow, usually square-shaped with a long verandah. A large hall led to adjacent dining and sitting rooms flanked by bedrooms with bathrooms attached. Depending on the availability of local building materials, some bungalows would be roofed with thatch, others with shingle. Those in the Nilgiris reminded Sir Richard Burton of modified cow-houses. In the Punjab wire-netted slits, 15 to 20 feet up, served as primitive windows. In an effort to get away from these unimaginative basic designs, a defiant flourish of Tuscan columns and classical arches would sometimes embellish flat-roofed, two-storeyed structures.

The interior decoration of houses had improved since the days when it was believed that too much furniture impeded the flow of air and attracted vermin. Imported carpets from England replaced the clean, smooth China matting which had been the normal floor covering. Snug chairs with coloured cushions, a piano and a billiard table, flowers in the fireplace and stencilled patterns on the bare, white walls were all designed to recreate the familiar surroundings of an English home. However, accommodation could still be spartan in Victorian times. The young subaltern's two-roomed bungalow made few concessions to comfort: a table, a couple of chairs, a hard sofa, a bed and perhaps a scattering of skins on the floor. The bachelors who congregated in 'chummeries' had little more than their basic needs – a charpoy bed with its obligatory mosquito net and some cheap canvas chairs.

The daily routine of domestic life was largely shaped by the Indian climate with its three distinct seasons of cold weather, hot weather and rains. Early rising became habitual to take advantage of the cool air of the morning and afternoon siestas were not unusual. When the sun had gone down tatties were removed, doors and windows flung open and the perceptible drop in temperature gratefully appreciated. In the evening the band played in the Mall while the fashionable world displayed itself in carriages and on horseback. Coolies staggered under the weight of ladies taking the air in palaquins and tonjons. Dinner and perhaps a party were the concluding stages to the day. Three substantial meals – breakfast, lunch or tiffin and dinner – were

A dandy or kind of sedan chair at Mussoorie

prepared by servants who evidently considered it a dereliction of duty not to include mulligatawny soup, curry and rice and caramel custard.

A retinue of servants was an obligation that few Europeans could evade. Emily Eden was bewildered by the number of servants attached to her.

> An astonishingly agreeable khitmagar . . . and four others glide behind me whenever I move from one room to another: besides these, there are two bearers with a sedan at the bottom of the stairs, in case I am too idle to walk, but I have not trusted my precious person to their care yet. There is a sentry at my dressing room door, who presents arms when I go to fetch my pocket handkerchief, or find my keys.

During the viceroyalty of Lord Lytton, there were three hundred indoor servants, of whom a third were cooks, at Government House. All were dressed in magnificent uniforms and it was said that on one embarrassing occasion Lytton embraced his head jemadar, resplendent in gold and lace, mistaking him for a visiting raja. This unfortunate Viceroy could never escape their solicitude at Government House. He complained that 'if he opened the door there were ten jemadars in red-and-gold livery crouching on the threshold'; if he strolled along the corridors 'three unpronounceable beings in white and red nightgowns' pursued him; a discreet departure by the backdoor inevitably involved being 'stealthily followed by a tail of fifteen persons.'

This army of servants was to some extent the consequence of caste prohibitions which decreed that a person of one caste could not touch anything handled by a member of another caste nor perform any of his duties. So the functions of gardener, groom, grass-cutter, dog-keeper, water-carrier, door-keeper or watchman had to be carried out by different men. In this way even a modest household could accumulate thirty servants. In many homes a bond of mutual understanding and care would develop between servants and employers. Unfortunately the special relationship between a bachelor and his bearer seldom survived the former's marriage. The ayah or maid, because she was in the privileged position of knowing a great deal about her mistress's domestic and social affairs, enjoyed a special intimacy.

> She has quick and ready hands to fold, to arrange, to pilfer; she has quick eyes to read her mistress's mood, and to know when it is safe to launch on a moving tale, to beg for an advance of pay, or to communicate the gossip of the day that has percolated through the servants of the neighbouring bungalow.

Murray's *Handbook of India* (1859) refuted the allegation that Indian servants lacked loyalty and integrity.

> Indian servants are often bad, because they are badly treated. Pay them well, and treat them well, and, in general, they will be found more faithful and attached than English domestics.

Over the many years the British were in India there evolved a code of social and moral behaviour more rigid and authoritarian than anything these

expatriates had known in England. It was, for instance, a peculiar autumn ritual to drop visiting cards in the little box fastened to the gatepost of every house, and an invitation to dinner would not be issued unless such a card had been received. It was a breach of protocol not to join the local Club even if one had no intention of participating in its activities. Dressing for dinner, even in the midst of the jungle, was not a custom to be lightly abandoned. The British were just as caste-conscious as the Indians. The Indian Civil Service represented the cream of society followed in descending order of importance by the provincial civil service, the army and businessmen. These class distinctions were not solely the product of Victorian vanity. As far back as 1792 the rules for subscription dances at the Calcutta Theatre ordained 'that ladies be taken out to dance minuets according to the rank their husbands hold in the King's or Hon'ble Company's service.' The immutable rules of *Precedence in the East Indies* (1841) precisely defined the social hierarchy; everyone, of course, deferred to the Governor-General who was followed by the State Governors, the Chief Justices, the Bishops, the Commander-in-Chief, Members of the Supreme Council, Judges and lesser mortals. Val Prinsep in 1877 found it a closed society to the visitor.

> The new order of precedence has just been published, which, if some had their way, would have been taken down to second-class post-office clerks. In this new order everything is settled, as to India; but the visitor, however high his rank, has no precedence, except by courtesy. I do not find any mention of artists in this document either with or without Government commission, and I am in consequence frequently left out in the cold.

A typical dak bungalow

Before the introduction of the railways there were several choices of transportation. The oldest and most popular, the palanquin, was a sort of square box with projecting poles, borne on the shoulders of four or six men (Plate 64). The passenger reclined, if he could, on cushions, consoled by the grunts and groans of his porters as they staggered over uneven roads at about three to four miles an hour. A gharry, which Prinsep ridiculed as a cross between a four-wheel cab and a hearse, was drawn by two horses, and could accommodate two passengers who, if they could ignore the bumpy ride, could stretch out on the mattress provided. On long journeys both the palanquin and the gharry had relays of fresh men and horses posted along the route. Overnight stops were made at dak bungalows, one of the ubiquitous features of the Indian landscape, thoughtfully provided by the Government at intervals of ten to fifteen miles, although on less-frequented roads they could be forty to fifty miles apart. They were substantially-built houses with a number of reasonably clean rooms furnished very simply with beds, tables, chairs and a bath. Rickshaws, tonjons and jampans (the latter described by one suffer as 'a jolting, back-aching abomination') were used locally in towns and cantonments. Budgerows flaunting crudely-carved and brightly-coloured figure-heads, and equipped with a couple of cabins for passengers, sailed the main rivers until competition from the railways forced them out of business. Within a remarkably short space of time the railway system spread its tentacles throughout the country, boring through the hills and mountains, bridging broad rivers, building palatial stations and consolidating the control of the Raj. An Afghan poet was moved by both wonder and apprehension at this steam monster which 'has neither feet nor hands, and goes backwards as well as forwards. It is the invention of the English, and one of the signs which herald the last judgment.'

The railways made it so much easier for the British to escape from the intolerable heat of the plains to cool resorts in the hills and mountains. Hill stations at Simla, Darjeeling, Mussoorie, Naini Tal, Ranchi and Ootacamund suddenly came alive during the summer months: rooms were aired, dust sheets were taken off the furniture, rickshaws were freshly painted, reunion parties were arranged. The government with its officials, clerks and files reopened its offices in Simla, Kipling's 'great and gay capital of India', perched nervously on its steep ridge 7000 feet up in the Himalayas. Municipal buildings in a pastiche of Gothic and Tudor looked uncomfortably out of place against the snow-capped peaks of the Himalayas; among the pines and the deodars narrow, winding paths led to insubstantial wooden bungalows with corrugated iron roofs. Everyone was determined to enjoy himself and every evening the roads were blocked with jampans taking their passengers to yet another party or dinner. But such social functions began to pall when one was always confronted with the same menus and the same people. Women who outnumbered men in these hill stations had endless opportunities for casual flirtations, and it was not surprising that envy and intrigue ruined many a reputation in this 'haven of familiarity'. Despite the fact that the Viceregal Lodge had one of the best views of the Snowy Range few of its distinguished occupants really enjoyed Simla. It was the sheer monotony of living there that repelled Lord Curzon. 'It is like dining everyday in the housekeeper's room with the butcher and the lady's maid.' Lord Lytton (who thought it 'a mere bivouac'), on the other hand, admired Ootacamund spread over the Nilgiri Hills, even when he saw it in the rain. 'The afternoon was rainy and the road muddy, but such beautiful English rain, and delicious English mud.' And Macaulay, who had resolved not to like India, was entranced by 'Ooty' and his cottage there 'buried in laburnums, or something very like them, and geraniums which grow in the open air. . . The vegetation of Windsor Forest or Blenheim spread over the mountains of Cumberland.'

At the end of the rainy season the hill stations became deserted once more as people returned to the cities, towns and remote settlements. Outside the cities were the cantonments for military personnel living a self-contained existence. Differing only in size, they were laid out in the same broad avenues with the officers' white bungalows set in neat squares of turf or dusty garden. Just beyond the boundaries of the cantonment there was

Camel transport at Lahore in 1885

usually an improvised race-course. Horse-racing had many devotees. In May 1798 the Court of Directors of the East India Company admonished the Government of India for allowing eight races to take place on a Sunday. The Bengal Jockey Club was formed in 1803 and even in precipitous Simla room was found for a hair-raising race-course at Annandale. At Gulmarg, nearly 9000 feet up in the Himalayas, golf was resolutely played by the fanatical. The sound of ball on cricket bat was first heard in Calcutta in 1804. For the more athletic and energetic there was usually the hunt and the pack of hounds that chased jackals in the absence of foxes. Pig-sticking called for courage as well as stamina. Big game could be stalked in the jungles and everywhere birds were easy targets. Well-stocked rivers surrounded by magnificent scenery were open to all fishermen.

India was paradise for the outdoor man; the sedentary and middle-aged had to seek other means of relaxation. At the Club, which was the focal point for all sociable people, one could dine, drink, gossip, play cards or billiards, dance exhausting lancers, quadrilles, waltzes and polkas or even borrow a book from its small library. Music had its ardent performers. Tableaux, charades and fancy-dress balls were popular with the young. Formal dinner parties were, for many people, something of a strain. 'We have been to one or two large dinner-parties rather grand, dull and silent' wrote Miss Julia Thomas from Madras in the 1830s.

> People talk a little in a very low voice to those next to them, but one scarcely ever hears any topic of general interest started except steam navigation. . .
> After dinner the company all sit round in the middle of the great gallery-like rooms, talk in whispers, and scratch their mosquito bites.

Theatre-going was a welcome relief from such ordeals, more relaxed and casual. Before the close of the eighteenth century two professional theatres had been established in Calcutta. Amateur theatricals were always the high spot of Simla life; up country (in the mofussil) officers and men of the regiments enjoyed performing on an improvised stage and a beefy soldier in a woman's dress was guaranteed always to raise a laugh.

The novelist Maud Diver viewed 'amateur theatricals and the military man on leave' as the greatest threat to 'the grass widow in the Hills.' Respectability became an obsession among the British in India, especially after the missionaries and memsahibs had got a firm hold. No doubt pondering biblical precepts in uncomfortable cantonments and lonely bungalows fostered the pervasive sense of sin. Murray's *Handbook for India* (1859) warned the traveller that 'in the tropics, licentious indulgence is far more dangerous and destructive than in Europe.' Misconduct, however, was probably no more prevalent in India than in Britain; the difference was that in India it was difficult to keep it secret. One commentator of the nineties, who seemed to speak from personal experience, remarked: 'Nowhere possibly in

the world are the passions of human nature laid so open for dissection as they are in the remote hill stations.' Lord Lytton made fun of the public parade of piety in a letter to Lady Salisbury in 1876:

> I envy you the pleasure of living among so many naughty people. Our own social surroundings here are so grievously good. Members of the Council and heads of departments hold prayer meetings at each other's houses thrice a week, and spend the rest of their time in writing spiteful minutes against each other. The young ladies are not allowed to dance lest they dance to perdition; and I believe moonlight picnics were forbidden last year by order of the Governor-General in Council lest they should lead to immorality. I wish I could report that our Empire was as well guarded as our piety.

There were comparatively few Englishwomen in India in the eighteenth century notwithstanding the attractions of ensnaring a rich husband. Captain Thomas Williamson's *East India Vade-mecum* (London, 1810) revealed 'that the number of European women to be found in Bengal and its dependencies cannot amount to two hundred and fifty; while the European male inhabitants of respectability, including military officers, may be taken at about four thousand.' In such circumstances it was not surprising that this surplus of bachelors sought to ease their frustrations by taking Indian mistresses; one elderly military acquaintance of Captain Williamson had

A tramcar in Bombay in the 1890s

sixteen! When asked by a friend how he coped with such a large number he replied affably: 'I give them a little rice, and let them run about.' This aged profligate wasted no time in courting a young woman, fresh from Europe, who firmly resisted his attentions when asked by a friend: 'Pray, my dear, how should you like to share a sixteenth of Major —— ?' Some women who found it difficult to decline a tempting offer of marriage soon regretted their impetuosity. One newlywed, writing to her cousin in 1779, revealed her disenchantment with the matrimonial state.

> I have obtained that for which I came out to India – a husband; but I have lost what I left behind me in my native country – happiness. Yet my husband is rich, as rich, or richer, than I could desire; but his health is ruined, as well as his temper, and he has taken me rather as a convenience than a companion.

Julia Thomas in one of her long letters from Madras was convinced that India was 'the paradise of middle-aged men.'

> While they are young, they are thought nothing of – just supposed to be making or marring their fortunes, as the case may be; but at about forty, when they are 'high in the service', rather yellow and somewhat grey, they begin to be taken notice of, and called 'young men'. These respectable persons do all the flirtation too in a solemn sort of way, while the young ones sit by, looking on, and listening to the elderly gentlefolks discussing their livers instead of their hearts.

The allure of a fortune, gracious living and servants, even at the expense of marrying a man past his prime, was an attraction that many women who flocked to India at the beginning of the cold weather season could not resist. This annual flood of females dedicated to scooping up husbands was known most appropriately as the Fishing Fleet. Once their husbands were securely netted, they quickly adapted to the conventions of domestic life in the tropics. They usually separated into two factions – the wives of civilians and officers viewing each other with suspicion and envy. They paid a great deal of attention to the niceties of social distinctions in their local aristocracy, endlessly discussing the shortcomings of the servants, the promotion of their husbands, and the education of their children in England. The memsahib has often been portrayed as the embodiment of the worst of middle-class prejudices but this is a generalization to which there were many exceptions. They did not have the monopoly of the arrogance and intolerance attributed to them. They were at a serious disadvantage in a male-dominated society where there was little opportunity of meeting Indian women, who were usually in purdah. Where it was possible for wives to help their husbands, usually civilians posted to remote stations, they frequently became friendly with Indian families and developed an abiding affection for India.

The supremacy of the British Raj was affirmed in a pageant of mediaeval grandeur on the plains just outside Delhi on 1 January 1877. The occasion was the proclamation of Queen Victoria as Empress of India, delivered with pomp and panache. Princes and chiefs from all over India came to pay homage to their Queen. The processional route, choked with richly caparisoned elephants, camel carriages, palanquins, tongas and gharries, was lined by soldiers in the distinctive uniforms of many famous regiments. The Viceroy's elephant perversely kept halting so that the cavalcade took three hours to cover the six miles to the arena. As the Viceroy in the light blue and silver robes of the Order of the Star of India mounted the throne beneath its conical canopy surmounted by the imperial crown, massed bands played vigorously and loudly. The Chief Herald, almost eclipsing the Viceroy in his multi-coloured tabard, read the Proclamation. Muslims lined up beneath their green banners patiently listened to the Foreign Secretary read it all again in Urdu. The artillery firing their salvoes in salute almost caused a stampede of the elephants. Then Lord Lytton rose to read a speech which practically no one heard. After three rousing cheers for the Queen Empress the Imperial Assemblage dispersed. Just six weeks later Val Prinsep, travelling alone in Marwar, and acutely conscious he was the only white man within a radius of thirty miles, thoughtfully mused. 'Truly the British Raj is a wonderful thing: if we have not won the native love, we have gained his respect or inspired him with a wholesome fear.' That was very much an imperial sentiment in accord with the spirit of the times, and it was that conviction which persuaded generations of Britons to dedicate their lives to the service of India, the jewel in the crown of the British Empire.

Plate 61 The Viceroy's elephants. When the Governor-General, Lord Dalhousie, tried to replace his state howdah 'of wood painted like a street cab' with a grander one of silver he was accused of reckless extravagance. The Lieutenant-Governors of the Punjab continued to use elephants for touring outlying districts long after the Viceroys had resigned themselves to travelling by train. One unfortunate Lieutenant-Governor, Sir Henry Durand, lost his life in 1871 when his elephant's howdah was crushed under an archway.

Plate 62 Drawing-room tent at Gwalior provided for Lord Elgin's staff during his Vice-regal tour in the autumn of 1895. The British in India usually lived well and were entertained in style. 'It is a perpetual astonishment to travellers to note the scale of living of every Englishman employed in India, in however mean a capacity,' remarked the Viceroy Lord Ripon. 'The enormous palaces of governors and lieutenant-governors, their country houses, their residences in the hills, their banquets and entertainments, their retinue of servants, their carriages and horses, their special trains on their journeyings, their tents, their armies of retainers and camp followers – these are only samples of the universal profusion.'

Plate 63 A camel carriage used during the visit of the Viceroy to Bhopal in November 1899. Government House in Lahore maintained a state camel carriage right up to the Second World War. It was not a popular form of travel with guests, who found it hard to endure the overwhelming odour of a team of these beasts.

Plate 64 A palanquin and its ▷ passenger in the 1860s. Until the mid-nineteenth century most European households in India had a palanquin and a team of bearers. It was the most common form of transport for long journeys and passengers usually had very positive opinions on its standard of comfort. One Victorian lady surprisingly thought it less tiring than a carriage, 'being able to sit up or lie down at pleasure, with plenty of room.' Sir Richard Burton, on the other hand, was decidedly less than enthusiastic: 'Between your head and the glowing sun, there is scarcely half an inch of plank, covered with a thin mat, which ought to be, but never is, watered. After a day or two you will hesitate which to hate most, your bearers' monotonous, melancholy grunting, groaning chaunt, when fresh, or their jolting, jerking, shambling, staggering gait when tired.' (See p. 79).

84

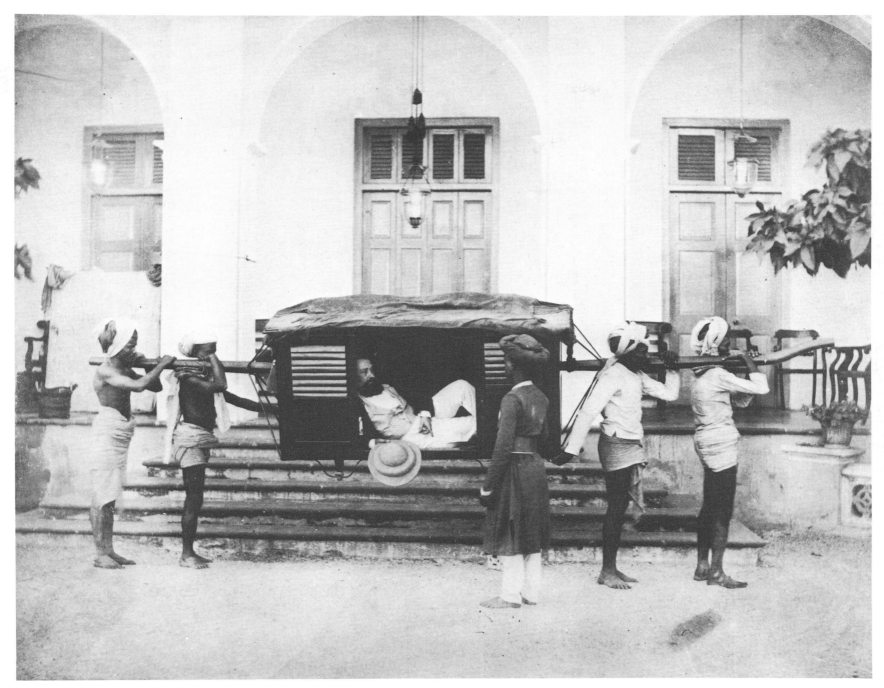

Simla cen...
Post...and Mall alo...

Plate 65 The Mall, the principal thoroughfare of Simla, with the post office on the left and the tower of Christchurch on the right; the thickly-wooded hill behind is Jakko, a favourite spot for morning and evening walks (*see p. 79*). Murray's *Handbook for Travellers* (1891) in extolling Simla's views and amenities warned that 'a number of people have been killed by falling over precipices at this station, and many more have had narrow escapes of their lives.'

Plate 66 Barnes Court in 1884, formerly the residence of the Commander-in-Chief in India and later of the Lieutenant-Governor of the Punjab. With its Tudor-style black and white architecture and carefully tended gardens it would not be out of place in the stockbroker belt of the Surrey countryside.

Plate 67 A picnic for the Viceregal staff at Simla in 1891. 'I was saying to my neighbour,' wrote Lady Dufferin from Simla in 1885, 'that one never was allowed to "rough it" in India, and that a picnic in our sense of the term seemed to be quite unknown here. . . I suppose that if we will dine out of doors. . . [it will be] with tables, and chairs, and silver, and every luxury that we are accustomed to at home.'

Plate 68 A view of Naini Tal ▷ in Kumaun, the summer residence of the Governor of the United Provinces. It was developed as a popular resort in the 1840s by the British, who built their houses around the sides of the thickly-wooded valley. Its principal feature is a pear-shaped lake, about two miles in circumference. This photograph, taken by Samuel Bourne in the 1860s, shows how he could skilfully manipulate his composition to give depth to his photograph. Water and its reflections were favourite features of his photographs.

Plate 69 Servants at work. A carefully arranged composition by W.W. Hooper, who served in the Madras Light Cavalry from 1858 until his retirement in 1896. Although only an amateur photographer he displayed the dedication and skill of a professional (*see p. 65*).

90

Plate 70 What could be more pleasant that a light lunch out of doors, followed by drinks served by attentive servants! A photograph of 1882.

Plate 71 A house at Darjeeling, one of the many hill stations where British-style architecture predominated.

Plate 72 Rowing at Poona. Lord Ripon dismissed the town as 'an uninteresting place, without a vestige of Eastern colour', but its position 2000 feet up in the Deccan plain, its pleasant climate and the opportunity to follow many outdoor pursuits made Poona very popular with the British. The river was dammed so that boating could be enjoyed for most of the year.

Plate 73 Wildfowlers, photographed by W.W. Hooper. This is a print that calls to mind similar subjects and equally sensitive treatment of some of the Victorian Fen photographs of the East Anglian photographer P.H. Emerson.

Plate 74 A leisurely game of croquet, which was very popular in the 1860s, at Murree, a hill station north of Rawalpindi.

Plate 75 Photograph by Samuel Bourne of goods being landed near the Customs House at Calcutta in the 1860s. The port is reached after 125 miles of very tortuous river navigation. The first dock was established in 1780 and, after the devastation caused by the cyclone of 1864, the port facilities were greatly improved. Today the serious silting of the River Hooghly prevents any large ships berthing there. The river has always been an integral part of the life of the city; for years the British used it to escape to their country houses at Chowringhee; the Governor-General left Calcutta by it in his state barge on his tours up-country; and Indians have always bathed in its sacred waters, which at the time of Durga Puja are full of bobbing images of the goddess drifting in the direction of the sea.

Plate 76 The Bhore Ghat reversing station on the Great Indian Peninsula line from Bombay to Poona. The main obstacle to extending the line from Bombay to Madras was a formidable mountain range, the Western Ghats, which flanks the western seaboard of the sub-continent. The Bhore Ghat, which rises to 2027 feet above sea level was selected as the most suitable route. Work began in 1856 and casualties were heavy among the labour force of thirty to forty thousand men. Twenty-five tunnels and twenty-two bridges had been constructed when this section of the line was eventually opened in 1863. It is one of the most impressive feats of Victorian railway engineering.

Victoria Station, Bombay

Plate 77 India's equivalent of St Pancras Railway Station in London is the Victoria Terminus, opened in Bombay in 1887. As an impressive building was required for the headquarters of the Great Indian Peninsula Railway, the architect, F.W. Stevens, produced a vigorous pastiche of Indo-Islamic and Venetian Gothic styles, dressed in a wealth of carved stone, iron and brasswork, stained-glass windows and glazed tiles. Robert Byron writing in the *Architectural Review* in 1931 castigated Bombay as 'that architectural Sodom'. He believed that 'the nineteenth century devised nothing lower than the municipal buildings of British India. Their ugliness is positive, daemonic.' Tastes and opinions have now completely changed. Today Bombay is regarded as having some of the finest Gothic Revival buildings anywhere in the world.

Plate 78 Barrackpore, the Viceroy's country residence some fifteen miles from Calcutta, was begun by Lord Wellesley in the early years of the nineteenth century and enlarged by the Marquis of Hastings. Successive Viceroys and their consorts sought to recreate an English country estate in the house and the grounds, which were landscaped and embellished with a temple, a terrace walk, Italian and rose gardens, a bamboo tunnel and the Gothic ruin that can be seen in this photograph taken by Samuel Bourne in the 1860s.

Plate 79 South Park Street Cemetery in Calcutta. Photographed by Frederick Fiebig in the early 1850s. Life was always precarious and frequently short for Europeans in India; if they were not carried off by fever, they fell victim to drink and other social excesses. This celebrated cemetery in Calcutta was opened in 1767 and its stuccoed mausolea designed as classical temples, obelisks and pyramids soon gave it the appearance of a city of the dead. Kipling said, 'The tombs are small houses. It is as though we walked down the streets of a town, so tall they are and so closely do they stand.' These packed cemeteries and the solitary graves which can be seen all over India are the most poignant and in many ways the most significant record of the days of the British Raj.